CELEBRATING THE PEOPLES AND · · CIVILIZATIONS OF AFRICA™

THE

DOGON

OF WEST AFRICA

Christine Cornell

The Rosen Publishing Group's
PowerKids Press™
New York

Published in 1996 by The Rosen Publishing Group, Inc.
29 East 21st Street, New York, NY 10010

First Edition

Book design: Kim Sonsky

Photo credits: Cover © Eric L. Wheater; pp. 4, 12 © Phyllis Galembo; pp. 7, 16, 19 © Eliot Elisofon/Eliot Elisofon Photographic Archives, National Museum of African Art, Smithsonian Institution; pp. 8, 11, 15, 20 © Jeffrey Jay Foxx.

Cornell, Christine.
    The Dogon of West Africa / Christine Cornell.
        p.   cm. — (Celebrating the peoples and civilizations of Africa)
    Includes index.
    Summary: Describes the history and customs of the Dogon, who live in Mali and Burkina Faso.
    ISBN 0-8239-2331-2
    1. Dogon (African people)—Juvenile literature. [1. Dogon (African people)] I. Title. II. Series.
DT551.45.D64C67 1996
966.2'0049635   96-18272
                                                                                                            CIP
                                                                                                            AC

Manufactured in the United States of America

CONTENTS

WHO ARE THE DOGON?

The **Dogon** (DOH-gon) are a West African people with a rich culture of art and thought. The Dogon believe that humans are the most important part of the **universe** (YOO-nih-vers). They also believe that knowledge comes through a lifetime of learning. Hundreds of years ago, most Europeans still thought the sun revolved around the earth. But the Dogon already believed that the sun was the center of the **solar system** (SO-ler SIS-tim). The beautiful art and culture of the Dogon draw many tourists to their land.

◀ People travel from all over the world to see the Dogon dance wearing their beautiful masks.

WHERE DO THE DOGON LIVE?

Many Dogon live among the **Bandiagara Cliffs** (BAN-dee-uh-GAR-uh KLIFS). These huge **sandstone** (SAND-stoan) cliffs stretch for 120 miles. At times they are 1,000 feet tall. The land on top of the cliffs is flat. At the bottom of the cliffs stretch vast, sandy plains. It is hot and dry in this part of West Africa. It doesn't rain very often.

Many Dogon grow crops in fields at the foot of the cliffs. ▶

MALI AND BURKINA FASO

There are about 400,000 Dogon people. They live in two countries: **Mali** (MAH-lee) and **Burkina Faso** (ber-KEE-nuh FAH-so). The Dogon live in the southern part of Mali and the northern part of Burkina Faso.

Mali and Burkina Faso are countries where people from North and West Africa come to buy and sell their products. There are many markets along the trade routes in these countries. Many Dogon sell their cloth at markets like these.

◀ There are many markets in Mali and Burkina Faso.

DOGON HOUSES

The Dogon use stones and earth mixed with water to build their houses. The Dogon build their homes to look something like humans.

Most Dogon houses don't have windows. The only openings are the doorway and a hole in the roof. Some of the houses have flat roofs. In those houses, a ladder leads up through the hole to the roof. When it is not raining, the whole family climbs up the ladder and sleeps on the roof.

The Dogon have buildings in many shapes. Some are shaped like cones. ▶

THE HOGON

The *hogon* (HOH-gon) is the leader of a Dogon group. There is one *hogon* for every three or four villages.

In the past, the *hogon* held great power. The Dogon believed that the *hogon* could control the seasons and the movement of the stars. They believed that he had the spirit of the whole universe inside him. The *hogon* also had important religious duties. Many Dogon still respect the powers of the *hogon*. But the *hogon* doesn't have as much power as he once did.

◄ The Dogon still look to their leaders, such as the *hogon*, for answers to their problems.

13

POTS, CLOTH, AND BASKETS

Instead of buying their cooking pots at a store, many Dogon still make them out of clay. Some of these pots are huge.

The Dogon also weave their own cloth and make their own clothing. The women spin thread from cotton grown in the fields. The men weave the thread into beautiful cloth.

Men also make strong baskets out of a type of reed called cane and from the huge leaves of palm trees.

Dogon women use the huge baskets that the men ▶
weave to carry goods to and from the market.

MASKS

The Dogon are famous for their beautifully carved and painted wooden masks called *imina* (ih-MEE-nuh). These masks are very important to the Dogon. They believe the masks have **nyama** (NYA-muh), or life force. All living things, such as plants, animals, and humans, have *nyama*. There are over 65 kinds of masks. Some are made to look like animals. Some are meant to be other African peoples. Some *imina* are worn by dancers who dance on stilts. One of the most special masks is called "the tree." It's 12 feet tall!

◄ Dogon carvers carefully carve masks for different ceremonies.

ANCESTORS

Young Dogon men wear masks during a special ceremony called the *dama* (DAH-muh). This is a special dance done every 10 or 15 years. It honors the **ancestors** (AN-ses-terz).

Before the ceremony, the men put their masks on in secret so that no one can tell who they are. Then they march to the village square. Musicians play flutes and drums. The young men do their spinning dances for the rest of the people in the village.

The Dogon have different dances that celebrate special days. ▶

GRIOTS

A very important person to the Dogon and many other peoples of West Africa is the **griot** (GREE-oh). A griot is a storyteller, a musician, and a poet. He is the person who remembers the history of the Dogon people. Through his stories, poems, and songs, he passes this knowledge on to his listeners. The griot travels from village to village bringing news and information. It is very exciting when the griot comes. The entire village gathers round to hear him perform and to learn what is going on in other places.

◀ Dogon children usually tell the rest of the village that the griot has arrived.

THE DOGON TODAY

The Dogon still grow almost everything they eat. They still wear their beautiful masks and perform their amazing dances. Many Dogon now leave their villages to live and work in cities. They often send money home to their families. They also send presents, such as T-shirts and sunglasses. The Dogon have combined their culture with many modern ideas.

GLOSSARY

ancestor (AN-ses-ter) Relative who lived before you.

Bandiagara Cliffs (BAN-dee-uh-GAR-uh KLIFS) Huge sandstone cliffs in West Africa.

Burkina Faso (ber-KEE-nuh FAH-so) Country in West Africa.

dama (DAH-muh) Ceremony that honors Dogon people who have died.

Dogon (DOH-gon) A people who live in West Africa.

griot (GREE-oh) Historian and carrier of news in many West African cultures.

hogon (HOH-gon) Leader of Dogon villages.

imina (ih-MEE-nuh) Famous wooden masks of the Dogon.

Mali (MAH-lee) Country in West Africa.

nyama (NYA-muh) Life force.

sandstone (SAND-stoan) Rock made from hardened sand.

solar system (SO-ler SIS-tim) The sun and all the planets that revolve around it.

universe (YOO-nih-vers) All things that exist.

INDEX